SECRETS OF THE ANIMAL WORLD

BEARS
Animals That Hibernate

by Isidro Sánchez
Illustrated by Gabriel Casadevall and Ali Garousi

Gareth Stevens Publishing
MILWAUKEE

For a free color catalog describing Gareth Stevens' list of high-quality books and multimedia programs, call 1-800-542-2595 (USA) or 1-800-461-9120 (Canada). Gareth Stevens Publishing's Fax: (414) 225-0377. See our catalog, too, on the World Wide Web: http://gsinc.com

The editor would like to extend special thanks to Jan W. Rafert, Curator of Primates and Small Mammals, Milwaukee County Zoo, Milwaukee, Wisconsin, for his kind and professional help with the information in this book.

Library of Congress Cataloging-in-Publication Data

Sánchez, Isidro.
    [Oso. English]
    Bears: animals that hibernate / by Isidro Sánchez ; illustrated by Gabriel Casadevall and Ali Garousi.
        p.   cm. – (Secrets of the animal world)
    Includes bibliographical references and index.
    Summary: Describes the physical characteristics, habitat, behavior, and life cycle of these powerful mammals, who live on most of Earth's continents.
    ISBN 0-8368-1636-6 (lib. bdg.)
    1. Bears–Juvenile literature. [1. Bears.] I. Casadevall, Gabriel, ill. II. Garousi, Ali, ill. III. Title. IV. Series.
    QL737.C27S2513   1997
    599'.78–dc21   96-46921

This North American edition first published in 1997 by
Gareth Stevens Publishing
1555 North RiverCenter Drive, Suite 201
Milwaukee, Wisconsin 53212 USA

This U.S. edition © 1997 by Gareth Stevens, Inc. Created with original © 1993 Ediciones Este, S.A., Barcelona, Spain. Additional end matter © 1997 by Gareth Stevens, Inc.

Series editor: Patricia Lantier-Sampon
Editorial assistants: Diane Laska, Rita Reitci

Printed in the United States of America

1 2 3 4 5 6 7 8 9 01 00 99 98 97

CONTENTS

THE GREATEST CARNIVORE ON EARTH

Where bears live

Bears are mammals that belong to the scientific order Carnivora. They live on four continents: North America, South America, Europe, and Asia. Polar bears live in the Arctic region, an area that is covered in ice and snow almost all year round. Other species live in warmer climates.

Bears also inhabit certain more southerly regions, but always within mountainous areas, such as the Pyrenees or the Cantabrian mountains.

The polar bear is one of the largest carnivores in the world. It is an excellent swimmer, and it feeds mainly on seals.

Two species of bears live in the southern hemisphere, in the jungles and rain forests of South America and Asia.

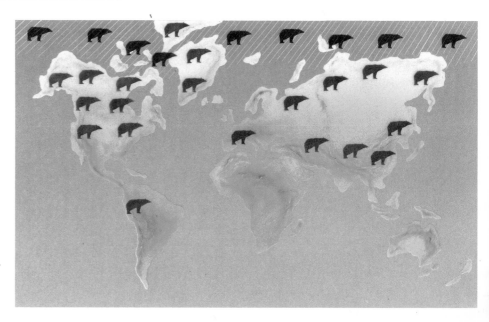

There are seven species of bears. The largest bears inhabit the northernmost regions of Earth, while the smaller ones live in southern Asia and South America.

The onset of winter

Like all other mammals, the bear is a warm-blooded animal. This means that the internal temperature of its body is always the same. Even though it is extremely cold in the northern forests and icy tundra, the bear maintains a constant body temperature.

The bear also has other ways of keeping warm. It has a heavy coat of hair, with a thick layer of fat underneath. This layer

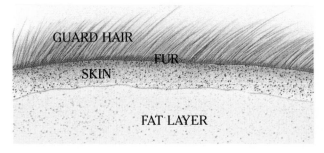

The thick layer of fat below the skin keeps the bear warm while it hibernates during the winter months.

prevents the escape of body heat and keeps out the cold.

Bears also hibernate in winter to help conserve their energy during a time when food is scarce.

The bear's thick coat of hair protects it from the cold.

Bear species

The polar bear is one of the largest carnivorous animals in the world. The male, or boar, can weigh over 1,765 pounds (800 kilograms) and stand over 8 feet (2.5 meters) tall. The female bear, or sow, is smaller. The polar bear lives in the Arctic, but sometimes travels south. The brown bear measures up to 6.5 feet (2 m) tall. Brown bears live in the United States, Canada, and Europe. The grizzly bear of the western United States is related to the giant brown bear of Alaska. The American black

GRIZZLY
BEAR

HIMALAYAN
BLACK BEAR

MALAYAN
SUN BEAR

POLAR
BEAR

SPECTACLED
BEAR

TIBETAN, or
BLUE, BEAR

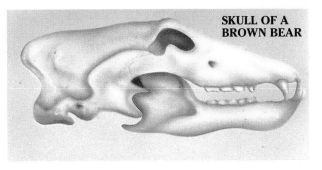

SKULL OF A
BROWN BEAR

*Bears have large skulls and brains.
Only the chimpanzee and the
elephant have brains that are larger
than the bear's.*

AMERICAN
BLACK BEAR

bear, smaller than the brown
bear, lives in North American
forests. The Himalayan black
bear has a long snout and eats
insects. Its fur is dark, with a
white U-shape on its chest. The
spectacled bear lives in South
America. It is small with dark
fur and white markings around
its eyes. It climbs trees and
builds nests in the branches.
The smallest bear, at about
3.2 feet (1 m) tall and weighing
about 132 pounds (60 kg), is
the Malayan sun bear. It has a
yellow half-moon on its chest.

*A wide variety of bear species
inhabit Earth. These are just a
few examples.*

BROWN
BEAR

INSIDE THE BEAR

The bear is a mammal with a large head, strong neck, and powerful limbs. Each of its feet and paws has five sharp claws. Many bears use their claws to climb trees by digging them into the bark. Although most bears live on the ground, they are comfortable in water, where they catch fish to eat.

AN INSULATING LAYER
The bear has a thick layer of fat under the skin that protects the animal against wet and cold.

INTESTINES

KIDNEY

LIVER

HIP

URINARY BLADDER

FEMUR

A WATERPROOF COAT
A layer of soft waterproof fur, located between the skin and the guard hair, keeps the bear's skin from getting wet when the animal swims.

STOMACH

FIBULA

TIBIA

WALKING STYLE
The bear can stand upright on its hind legs, but it walks on all fours. It moves its front and hind legs on one side at the same time, then moves the two on the other side.

FOOT BONES

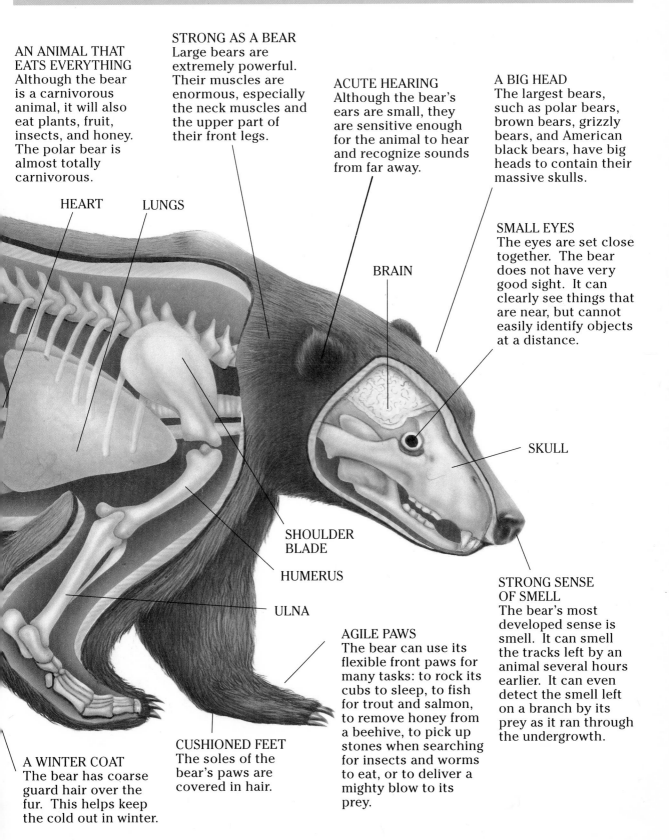

AN ANIMAL THAT EATS EVERYTHING
Although the bear is a carnivorous animal, it will also eat plants, fruit, insects, and honey. The polar bear is almost totally carnivorous.

STRONG AS A BEAR
Large bears are extremely powerful. Their muscles are enormous, especially the neck muscles and the upper part of their front legs.

ACUTE HEARING
Although the bear's ears are small, they are sensitive enough for the animal to hear and recognize sounds from far away.

A BIG HEAD
The largest bears, such as polar bears, brown bears, grizzly bears, and American black bears, have big heads to contain their massive skulls.

HEART

LUNGS

BRAIN

SMALL EYES
The eyes are set close together. The bear does not have very good sight. It can clearly see things that are near, but cannot easily identify objects at a distance.

SKULL

SHOULDER BLADE

HUMERUS

ULNA

AGILE PAWS
The bear can use its flexible front paws for many tasks: to rock its cubs to sleep, to fish for trout and salmon, to remove honey from a beehive, to pick up stones when searching for insects and worms to eat, or to deliver a mighty blow to its prey.

STRONG SENSE OF SMELL
The bear's most developed sense is smell. It can smell the tracks left by an animal several hours earlier. It can even detect the smell left on a branch by its prey as it ran through the undergrowth.

A WINTER COAT
The bear has coarse guard hair over the fur. This helps keep the cold out in winter.

CUSHIONED FEET
The soles of the bear's paws are covered in hair.

SLEEPING ALL WINTER LONG

Animals and hibernation

During winter, the cold is not the main threat to animals that live in cold regions of the world.

The most serious problem is lack of food. The snow covers everything in sight, and there is practically no vegetation. Even carnivores find it difficult to hunt their usual prey. Animals react to this difficulty in various ways. Some move on to another place where they can find more abundant sources of food. Birds do this when they migrate.

Other animals do not leave their habitat when winter arrives. Instead, they have adapted to surviving the cold by hibernation. Many mammals hibernate — small ones, such as hedgehogs and bats, and large ones, such as the bear.

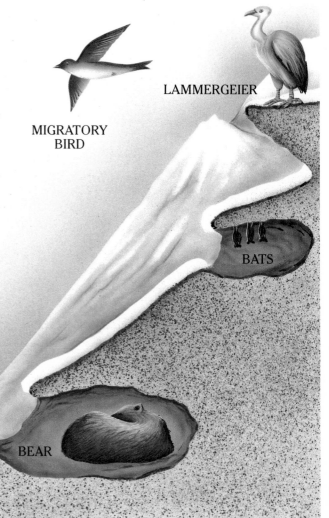

MIGRATORY BIRD

LAMMERGEIER

BATS

BEAR

MOLE

During winter, many birds migrate, although some, like the lammergeier, remain in their habitat. Many small and large mammals hibernate. Bears frequently wake up during their winter sleep.

that some animals sleep very deeply during winter?

As winter approaches, some animals — such as bears, bats, and hedgehogs — go into a state of hibernation.

The dormouse also hibernates. It curls up and remains totally still, so still that it looks like a ball of hair. Its body undergoes changes in order to use the least amount of energy. Its temperature goes down, its heart beats much more slowly, and it breathes much less frequently than normal.

Most hibernating animals do not sleep continuously. They usually get up once every two or three weeks, remain awake for a day or so, and then go back into hibernation.

Eating their fill

As winter approaches, bears prepare themselves for the lack of food and the cold weather.

At the beginning of autumn, the polar bear sets out to hunt. It uses a large piece of floating ice to carry it across open stretches of water until it finds a seal colony. Then the bear hunts as many seals as it can. Winter is near, and it will be difficult for the polar bear to find food.

The brown bear and the American black bear live in

The brown bear and the American black bear fish with their claws in mountain rivers. Their favorite fish are trout and salmon.

habitats containing a variety of food, such as roots, grass, leaves, fruit, insects, squirrels, and small wild boar.

This polar bear breaks the ice away from the seal's hiding place with its powerful paws.

All bears have a sweet tooth except the polar bear, which cannot find honey in its habitat.

Bears are also experts at fishing. They scoop fish out of the water using their paws. Trout and salmon are their favorite fish. But bears love honey best. They tear the honeycomb open with their claws and eat the honey.

The food consumed by the bear before winter turns into fat. This fat accumulates under the skin and provides the bear with protection against the cold and with energy to survive a long winter.

Sleep and more sleep . . .

Despite the extreme Arctic cold, the male polar bears do not hibernate. Instead, the males roam the ice pack in search of prey, and the sows stay in dens dug into the snow. The cubs are born in the den. The sow cares for them by herself.

The brown bear and the black bear hibernate in caves and make beds of moss, grass, and dry leaves. During hibernation, the bear's body functions slow

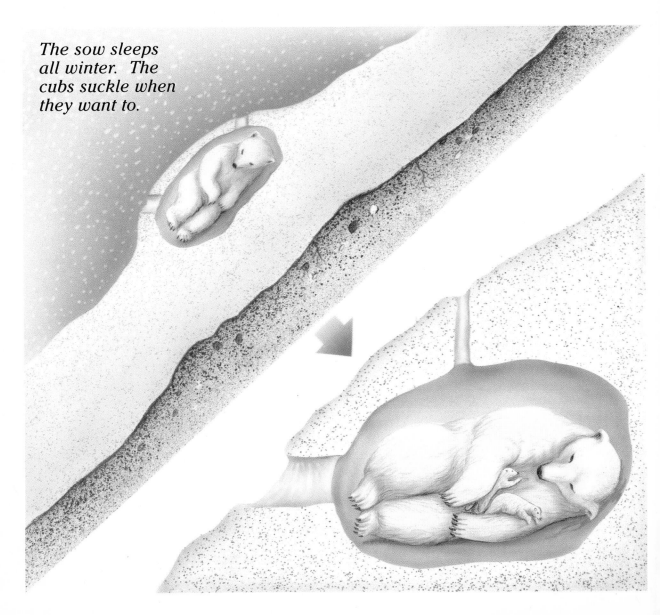

The sow sleeps all winter. The cubs suckle when they want to.

These American black bear cubs have spent their entire two months of life in the cave where they were born.

down, especially its heartbeat and respiration. Its body temperature also decreases. The bear's fat gives it enough energy to make up for the lack of food during winter.

Another feature of the bear's hibernation is its ability to "program" the birth of its young. After the male and female have mated, the fertilized ovum does not begin to develop until several months later. This way,

the cubs will not be born until the middle of winter, within the comfortable den, safe from the cold. The cubs are born while the mother is hibernating. She awakens only to break the umbilical cord with her teeth and then goes back to sleep. The cubs sleep most of the time and only wake up to suckle.

Ferocious hunger

When spring arrives in the Arctic and the ice floes begin to melt, the sow goes out hunting. Aside from being hungry, the bear also wants to show the cubs hunting techniques. So it catches more seals than it needs to eat.

After hibernation, other bear species, extremely thin after fasting for so long, also spend a lot of time eating. During this time, they eat plants because they are too weak to hunt.

The cubs continue to suckle from their mother until they are three months old. When they leave the den at the end of

Cubs are less hungry than their mother, for she has spent the entire winter without eating. But the cubs are eager to try new kinds of foods, such as fruit and insects.

winter, they immediately begin to dig up roots and grass and start eating snails and insect larvae. Later on, the cubs learn to hunt and fish.

One of the first things the polar bear does at the start of spring is to teach its cubs how to hunt seals.

that certain animals have "naps" that last several months?

In the same way that certain mammals hibernate in cold climates, other animals sleep the entire summer in hot climates.

This long "nap" is known as estivation, a light sleep that involves fewer changes in the animal's body than hibernation.

Estivation helps desert animals survive the heat and lack of water.

In some species, only the males sleep. There are also animals that sleep both in the summer and in the winter. Some other animals change their daily habits when summer arrives.

HOW BEARS LIVE

Best mother in the world

Bears live in small family groups, called sloths. Sloths include sows, newborns, and cubs.

   The family members always remain together, even when they are out hunting in the forest or on the ice pack. They also play together. Polar bear cubs slide down the ice until they are exhausted. When they are slightly older, they play-fight among themselves. The mother bear never lets her cubs stray far away. In times of danger, she can confront male bears twice her size. The cubs do not leave the family until they are two years old.

Mother bears are very affectionate. They take constant care of their cubs and never leave their side.

Most bears love to play. This polar bear cub enjoys sliding down a hill.

King of the ice and forest

The polar bear's only enemy among the other creatures that inhabit the icy waters of the polar north is the male walrus. Although the polar bear likes to hunt seals and female or young walruses, it will not confront a male walrus. This is because the male walrus has two sharp, powerful tusks. A polar bear will not even enter the water if a male walrus swims nearby.

Other bear species, especially the American black bear and the

This young American black bear is sure to lose against the puma, its greatest enemy.

brown bear, have few enemies in their forest habitat because they are strong and fierce. Only newborns and cubs are vulnerable to attacks by pumas — American wildcats.

With its long, powerful tusks, the male walrus is the polar bear's arch enemy.

Humans and bears

Humans hunted the polar bear for many years for its pelt, which was used to make fur coats. Agreements now exist to reduce or prohibit this practice.

Humans have also hunted the polar bear in self-defense. Small groups of hungry polar bears searching for food can invade Inuit settlements or approach some Canadian towns.

Inuit call the polar bear *nanook*, which means "great white bear," and they love and respect it. But a polar bear that approaches an Inuit village can

Bears can get angry very easily. But they do not normally attack people.

be very dangerous. The brown bear can also be aggressive, as can the grizzly bear. Most bear attacks on humans take place either because the bears are wounded or because they have been separated from their cubs.

Polar bears sometimes come into the towns of northern Canada in search of food in the garbage.

that polar bears play hide-and-seek with seals?

Arctic animals live in ice and snow. Since there is little vegetation, the only way to obtain food is by hunting other animals. Seals make holes in the ice for fishing. They remain in the water and stick their heads out to take in air. The polar bear, attracted by the seal's smell, begins a game of hide-and-seek. It covers several holes and then waits for the seal to come up for air out of a remaining uncovered hole. When a seal sticks its head out, the bear strikes a blow and gets its food.

PREHISTORIC BEARS

The cave bear

About 100,000 years ago, prehistoric humans lived alongside enormous animals that could stand over 13 feet (4 m) tall and weigh 2,200 pounds (1,000 kg) — the cave bears.

The cave bear was both prey and enemy to prehistoric humans. Humans hunted cave bears mainly for their skin — to

CLAW

REMAINS OF THE CAVE BEAR

The cave bear's skull was larger and longer than that of the brown bear. The claws were also bigger.

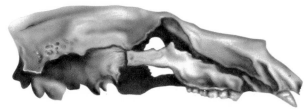

SKULL

The cave bear lived at the same time as prehistoric humans, with whom it competed for caves to live in.

use as protection against the extreme cold of that time.

Like humans, the bear found protection in caves. Sometimes a cave bear entered a cave occupied by humans. Then it was humans against bear for possession of the cave.

Protected by its thick fur, the cave bear adapted well to the intense cold of the ice age. It searched for food in the frozen wastelands and in the deep tracts of forest. In spite of its fierce appearance, the cave bear was an herbivore. It confronted humans only to defend itself.

Cavemen did not think twice about approaching the fearsome cave bear. The need to defend their families over-came any personal fears.

APPENDIX TO

SECRETS OF THE ANIMAL WORLD

BEARS
Animals That Hibernate

BEAR SECRETS

▼ **Covering its nose.** The polar bear has white or yellow fur with a touch of black at the tip of its nose. When it waits next to an ice hole for a seal to come up for air, the polar bear instinctively covers its nose so as not to give itself away. When an unsuspecting seal appears, the bear pounces.

▼ **Attentive mother.** If a mother bear and her cubs cross a stretch of open water, the mother swims in front, and the cubs form a chain by grabbing the tail of the bear in front.

▼ **A greedy bear.** To catch the termites it eats, the Himalayan black bear digs holes in their hills.

▼ Nests for bears. The spectacled bear, like several other species of bears, is an expert tree climber. It feeds off the fruit and leaves. The spectacled bear also builds large nests in the trees.

Excellent swimmers. The polar bear is an excellent swimmer. It can swim over 6.2 miles (10 km) without stopping. It swims by moving its front paws as if it were rowing. The polar bear is also good at diving.

1. The polar bear lives:
a) in the United Sates.
b) in the Arctic Circle.
c) in Antarctica.

2. To which family does the grizzly bear belong?
a) The brown bear family.
b) The polar bear family.
c) The Himalayan black bear family.

3. The bear's most developed sense is:
a) sight.
b) smell.
c) hearing.

4. Hibernation is:
a) a technique used by animals for adapting to the cold.
b) a type of food for winter.
c) a form of reproduction for mammals.

5. The polar bear's main enemy is:
a) the Arctic fox.
b) the penguin.
c) the male walrus.

6. The prehistoric bear was called:
a) the ice bear.
b) Ursus terribilis.
c) the cave bear.

The answers to BEAR SECRETS questions are on page 32.

GLOSSARY

abundant: plentiful; having a large amount.

adapt: to make changes or adjustments in order to survive in a changing environment.

aggressive: bold; eager to confront or engage in combat.

agile: nimble; able to move quickly or easily.

Arctic: the most northern area of Earth, centered on the North Pole and bordered on the south by the Arctic Circle at 60°30′ N latitude. The Arctic has long winters with extremely cold temperatures.

boar: a fully grown male bear; also a fully grown male swine.

carnivores: meat-eating animals.

colony: a community with members that live and work together.

confront: to face or meet aggressively, as in an argument or fight.

conserve: to use something carefully in such a way that it isn't hurt or used up.

continents: the large landmasses of Earth, which include Africa, Antarctica, Asia, Australia, Europe, North America, and South America.

cub: a young bear, wolf, or lion.

den: the shelter or lair of a wild animal.

detect: to notice or discover something.

estivation: the state of rest and inactivity that occurs for some animals in the heat of summer.

flexible: able to bend or move with ease.

habitat: the natural home of a plant or animal.

herbivores: animals that eat only plants.

hibernation: a state of rest or inactivity in which most bodily functions, such as heartbeat and breathing, slow down.

honeycomb: a structure of hexagonal (six-sided) wax cells built by bees in their hives. The bees store pollen, honey, and eggs in the honeycomb.

internal: located within or inside something.

Inuit: the people formerly called Eskimos, who live in the North American Arctic.

invade: to enter by force, sometimes in great numbers.

lack (*v*): to be in a condition of not having something that is needed.

larva: the wingless, wormlike form of a newly-hatched insect; in the life cycle of insects, amphibians, fish, and some other organisms, the stage that comes after the egg but before full development.

mammals: warm-blooded animals that have backbones. Female mammals produce milk to feed their young.

massive: heavy and solid; huge.

mate (*v*): to join together (animals) to produce young; to breed a male and a female.

migrate: to move from one place or climate to another, usually on a seasonal basis.

ovum: a small egg in an early stage of growth.

polar: relating to those regions of Earth centered around the north and south poles; these areas are very cold and icy.

prehistoric: something that lived or happened before people began to keep written records.

prey: animals that are hunted, captured, and killed for food by other animals.

prohibit: to forbid; to prevent from doing something.

puma: a large, powerful light brown cat found in western North America; also called cougar or mountain lion.

respiration: the act of breathing.

scarce: not having enough to meet a demand; insufficient.

snout: protruding nose and jaw of an animal.

sole: the bottom of a foot or hoof.

sow: a fully grown female bear.

species: animals or plants that are closely related and often similar in behavior and appearance. Members of the same species are able to breed together.

stray: to wander or roam; to move away from other members of a group.

suckle: to nurse; to draw milk from the mother's breast.

tundra: an area in Arctic regions that has no trees and very few other types of plants.

tusk: a long, pointed tooth that sticks out of the mouth. Male walruses and elephants have huge tusks.

umbilical cord: the lifeline that connects a baby to its mother.

undergrowth: the low growth on the floor of a forest, which includes saplings, shrubs, and small plants.

vulnerable: in a weak position; open to attack.

ACTIVITIES

◆ Visit a zoo or museum that has bear exhibits. What kinds of bears do you see? What parts of the world do these bears inhabit in the wild? Compare the sizes of the bears: draw pencil lines 1/2-inch (1.2-cm) apart across a sheet of paper, then draw lines 1/2-inch apart all the way down the paper. Each 1/2-inch represents a foot of the bear's measurement. With a crayon, make a rectangle the length and height of each bear, and fill it in with a color, like black, creamy yellow, or shades of brown. Next to each rectangle, write the name of the bear. Which bear is largest? Smallest? Which are nearly the same size?

◆ On a map of the world, outline areas inhabited by bears. Choose a color for each kind of bear and use crayons, pencils, or watercolors to color the area where that kind of bear lives. If more than one kind of bear inhabits that area, use alternating strokes of the bears' colors. Make a key by coloring a small patch along one side of the map and writing the name of the bear it represents beside it.

MORE BOOKS TO READ

Amazing Bears. Theresa Greenaway (Knopf Books for Young Readers)
Bear. Mike Down (Troll Communications)
The Bear Family. Dieter Betz (Morrow)
Bears. Donna Bailey (Raintree Steck-Vaughn)
Bears. Ian Stirling (Sierra)
Bears, Big and Little. Pierre Pfeffer (Young Discovery Library)
Bears and Their Forest Cousins. Annemarie Schmidt and
    Christian R. Schmidt (Gareth Stevens)
Black Bear Magic for Kids. Jeff Fair (Gareth Stevens)
The Everywhere Bear. Sandra C. Robinson (Roberts Rhinehart)
Polar Bears. Jenny Markert (Childs World)

VIDEOS

All About Bears. (National Film Board of Canada)
Bears! (Bullfrog Films)
Bears! Bears! Bears! (Adventure Productions)
The Bears Go Fishing. (Phoenix/BFA Films and Video)
Polar Bears and Their Frozen World. (Encyclopædia Britannica)

PLACES TO VISIT

Lincoln Park Zoo
2200 North Cannon Drive
Chicago, IL 60614

Metro Toronto Zoo
Meadowvale Road
West Hill, Ontario M1E 4R5

Auckland Zoological Park
Motions Road
Western Springs
Auckland 2, New Zealand

**Denver Zoological
    Gardens**
City Park
2300 Steele Street
Denver, CO 80205

Adelaide Zoo
Frome Road
Adelaide, South Australia
Australia 5000

The Mugga Lane Zoo
RMB 5, Mugga Lane
Red Hill
Canberra, A.C.T.
Australia 2609

Calgary Zoo
1300 Zoo Road
Calgary, Alberta
T2V 7E6

INDEX

Answers to BEAR SECRETS questions:
1. b
2. a
3. b
4. a
5. c
6. c